ENTER, F

MARK FORD

Enter, Fleeing

FABER & FABER

First published in 2018
by Faber & Faber Ltd
Bloomsbury House
74–77 Great Russell Street
London WC1B 3DA

Typeset by Hamish Ironside
Printed in England by Martins the Printers, Berwick-upon-Tweed

A CIP record for this book is available from the British Library

ISBN 978-0-571-33999-0

2 4 6 8 10 9 7 5 3 1

In memory of Karl Miller and Dan Jacobson

Acknowledgements

Acknowledgements are due to the editors of the following publications, in which some of these poems first appeared: *London Review of Books*, *New Walk*, *Oxford Poetry*, *Paris Review*, *Poetry*, *Poetry London*, *The Spectator*, *Times Literary Supplement*.

Contents

I

Show Time   5
Driveaway   8
Nairobi, 1963   10
Far-Fetched   11
Lagos, 1967   14
Aloft   15
In Loco Parentis   17
World Enough   18
Chicago, 1969   20
Enter, Fleeing   21
Tribal   23
Viewless Wings   24
Love Triangle   27
A Broken Appointment   28
Under the Lime Trees   29

II

Supply and Demand   35
Mickey Finn   36
Dark Matter   39
Mayhem   41
Colombo, 1970   43
Stigmata   44
Hong Kong, 1973   46
Daphne and Apollo   47
Bahrain, 1977   49
Fide et Literis   50
New York, 1982   53

Adrift   54
Brighton Rock   55
Oxford, 1985   56
Trial and Error   57

Notes   63

I

Again and again, in Shakespeare, in Calderón, battles fill the last act, and kings, princes, attendants and followers 'enter, fleeing'. The moment in which they become visible to spectators brings them to a standstill. The flight of the dramatis personae *is arrested by the stage. Their entry into the visual field of non-participating and truly impartial persons allows the harassed to draw breath, bathes them in new air. The appearance on stage of those who enter 'fleeing' takes from this its hidden meaning. Our reading of this formula is imbued with expectation of a place, a light, a footlight glare, in which our flight through life may be likewise sheltered in the presence of onlooking strangers.*

— WALTER BENJAMIN, 'One-Way Street'

Show Time

Tempus fugit every sundial
proclaims, yet over and over
time seems to swoon, or to expand, even
to grind
to a juddering halt
when I blog; a dreadful day
online, I think I mean, is a dreadful
day forever. My current
screensaver is a sniper's-
eye view of a traffic warden
leaning
back to photograph
an illegally parked car. Hatchet-
faced tax inspectors invade my dreams: 'We need
you to live,' they murmur, lips
nearing, even
brushing
my helpless ear.

In what
wrinkle, in what furrow
or fissure lurks
the longing to make the worst
happen? As if
I had conjured them, one
Halloween two hooded figures loomed
above me
on a bridge I was dawdling across
in downtown Boston; their cradled
half bricks crashed

con brio, with energy and purpose
into my swirling
stream of thoughts . . . treats
for the favoured few, endless
tricks for the others . . . travelling by water
is best because you n-n-n-n-never
have to go uphill . . .

              I lay
prone awhile . . . then, springing
to life, into action,
I fled. Something – my heart – boomed
and echoed like pursuing
footsteps on asphalt. *Leeeeeft*, a voice shouted
in a comic French accent, *erpp yer aass*. Laughter.
Don't stop don't stop
till you get enough! 'Are you', I recall
demanding of a friendly
paramedic as he shone his pencil torch
deep into my eyes, 'an electric light bulb, and
if so,
what wattage?' No one
I met seemed to know
about soldier ants, about how
their jaws, or maybe their claws, are used in Africa
to stitch up wounds.

              Discharged
with a warning, how quietly
I crept home through the mazy, moonlit
streets of Roxbury, avoiding
alleys and skips, my scars
stinging like unwisely
acquired tattoos. Halloween

was over. High
above rows of ghostly buildings
hollowed out
by descendants of the locust or the palmer-
or cankerworm, giant
Citgo and Exxon signs smiled
encouragement. Glancing
down, I noticed a red coin
of blood disfiguring
the left knee of my chinos – and thinking
this funny, I began to limp.

Driveaway

After we careered into a pick-up truck
At a crossroads near Kansas City, we slept
On picnic benches, or in the patched-up, dented car.
The black-gowned judge smiled at our outlandish attire.

We too, O Kansas City, were at a crossroads; we slept
Uneasily, occasionally touching, our dreams at cross-purposes.
The black-gowned judge smiled at our outlandish attire
Before drawling, 'Guess you two've gone about *as fer as you
    can go!'*

Uneasily, occasionally touching, our dreams at cross-purposes,
Here we were, driving from coast to coast, taking turns
To drawl, 'Guess you two've gone about *as fer as you can go!'*
Other times we'd softly murmur, 'Toto, I've a feeling we're not
    in Kansas anymore.'

Here we were, driving from coast to coast, taking turns
At admiring the landscape, until, one afternoon, I heard
You weeping, *'Toto . . . I've a feeling . . . we're NOT . . . in
    Kansas anymore . . .
We must be . . . over the rainbow.'*

I was the one admiring the landscape later that afternoon. All
    I heard
Was the song of the wheat fields rustling, and the swish of our
    tyres –
. . . we must be – we must be – we must be – over the rainbow . . .
As evening fell we approached St Louis.

The song of the wheat fields rustling and the swish of our
    tyres
Had lulled me gently to sleep.
As evening fell, and we approached St Louis
Sting woke me up, being venomous, on 'Every Breath You
    Take'.

I kept being lulled gently to sleep
Then dreaming of careering into a pick-up truck,
And Sting kept waking me up, and being venomous on
    'Every Breath You Take',
On picnic benches, in the patched-up, dented car.

Nairobi, 1963

Totally appalled,
my mother told
our cook that John
F. Kennedy had been *shot!* – and holding
up floury hands, he sighed
and smiled, and murmured, 'Soon,
bibi,' and went
on kneading dough.

Far-Fetched

Das ist der doux commerce!
— KARL MARX

Ay de mi – a pin-
prick of blood, scarcely
more than a pore
flaunting its friendship
with a vein; bright
as the flower
of the flame tree that stained
our drive, our lawn, and the roof
and bonnet of our white
Ford Taunus
red . . . in piercing, heat-
hazed dreams Tina
the Turkey, fattening for Christmas in the dust
of Kano, interrupts
her pecking to fix
me with a beady eye, to puff
her breast and shake
at me her scarlet
beak and wattles. 'The worse
it is, the better,' she cluck-clucks, *sotto
voce*, from somewhere
deep
inside the labyrinth
of my skull: 'On all
fours enter my unhappy coop, and lend
an ear: prolonged
and torrential storms will erode
the dirt I'm scratching in; the hand

that hurls the grain, and wields
the cleaver, and the rattan
carpet-beater, will change
before your eyes into a curved
and scaly
claw . . . Weep
with me for the doomed, for all short-winged
flightless birds, for the many
stragglers that the swirling waters
will pursue, and overwhelm . . . As I know
you know, beyond
this paling
scheming irregulars in tattered
fatigues prowl through the night, or gather
in clearings; *crackle –*
crackle – crackle – whoooosh! – the roar
of the flames from their bushfires
makes the roots
of my feathers shiver
and tingle . . . Should you
like a fool venture forth, beware of the pitter
and the patter of overgrown children
scurrying for cover, themselves
fully fledged, and resourceful
child-
catchers; and while I
scratch for fleas, and gobble
and gabble, can't
you hear the shrieking of anxious
and bewildered parakeets – *here I am, oh,*
oh, here I am! – in flight from the noise
and the smoke, their cries
putting words in your mouth, *oh here –*
here I am – send me! . . . How

far these far-
fetched facts must travel before
they buckle and fall, and how
s-s-s-softly they dissolve
in the wind . . . the wind, *ah oui, le vent
se lève*, and *en garde* –
en garde, my friend, for I see
you mean to pluck each speckled plume
from this heaving breast, to skewer
and season
and devour me . . . welladay, or rather
whoops! – for it appears
that one of these
rogue talons
has flashed towards the cornea
of your left eye, and nicked it,
so, and now
the right: and hence
our heart-to-heart, our sweet
sweet *commerce* is breaking
into a chaos of flame-
coloured filaments
hovering, and sinking
like fireflies, and the *rat-
a-tat-tat*
of rain
on corrugated iron . . .'

Lagos, 1967

'*Wait here!*' my mother commanded, white
with fury; then she set off in pursuit.

A man had snatched her bag, and was running
away with it.

Knees and carts and honking cars
obscured our view.

I guess she caught up with the robber, and wrestled
the bag back, vehemently

demanding, '*How dare you! – How
DARE you! –*

How dare you!'

Aloft

Trust me, or rather *text* me – I need
right now the winged
the divine
happiness of conception – *zhuuum* . . . recall
for me the lingering
aftershave of the one who hoisted
you high in the Country Club car park, and got sent
to jail for molesting
minors. Attach
a snap of the lonely peacock
of Holland Park, his beak
parted to scream, tail fan arced and quivering, dark
eye outraged . . . We turn
aside, then peer
inwards, composed
of insurgent, or of waning
Eros, of inconvenient aches and pimples, of DNA-
inflected dust.

*

An airport
is a delightful retreat for any mind grown weary
of the struggles of life. The vast expanse of sky, the shifting
architecture of the clouds, the dizzying colours
of the tail fins,
the beacons flashing on the runway, all
create a prism which is marvellously calculated
to entertain but not weary
the eye.

I like to think of uniformed pilots in cockpits surveying
flickering banks of instruments, of planes shuddering
into motion, ordered this way
and that by air traffic controllers sipping lukewarm coffee
in towers.

Above all there is a mysterious, aristocratic sort of
pleasure to be derived, by those who have themselves lost
all curiosity, all ambition, and now lean on their elbows
on the rail of the viewing deck, from contemplating the
arrivals and departures of those who still harbour belief
and purpose, who are still driven by the desire to travel,
or by

the urge

to enrich themselves.

*

Where are – I mean what happened to – my Junior
Jet Club Logbook and my framed
certificates awarded for having flown
25,000 miles – 50,000 miles –
75,000 miles – 100,000 miles –
after which we gave up counting
or they ran out of certificates?

In Loco Parentis

were some quite creepy men – one
used to lie down
on the dayroom floor, then get us all
to pile on top of him – and a basilisk-
eyed matron in a blue uniform with a watch
dangling
beneath her right
collarbone. *Thump thump*
thump went her footsteps, making
the asbestos ceiling tiles shiver, and me
want to hide, or run like a rabbit
in a fire . . .
                    What we lost, we lost
forever. A minor
devil played at chess
with us, forcing
the pieces to levitate
and hover, flourishing swords, in mid-air. I'd grasp
them now, the orotund bishop, the stealthy
knight, the all-
knowing queen,
but they dissolve
in my fingers, refuse
to return to the board, to their squares.

World Enough

Yo-ho! – haul high the Jack, or the Jolly
R-R-Roger, however
tattered and torn, but also
r-r-remove a pirate's
favourite letter, turning
friend to *fiend*, and *fright*
to *fight*! The Empire
was flummoxed, and dissolving
fast when we
set sail on the Seven Seas, late, late
buccaneers in quest
of whatever booty
remained: a retinue
of 'bearers', a bare-
footed gardener, lychees and lime juice and papaya
brought to us
on the veranda, a chauffeur
in a crisp
white shirt with pleats and pockets
and epaulettes . . . my sister
wept when 'David', an ageing, impassive servant
dismissed for getting 'filthy drunk'
on arak, returned, red-
eyed, to retrieve a cushion
he'd forgotten . . . I watched
him adjust
his bundle, rise, then stagger off again, his wispy
grey hair coming loose
from its bun . . . no more
dusting of ebony heads

from Nigeria, onyx elephants, sphinxes carved
out of soapstone; our gaudy, bug-eyed
demon masks, or the glass
protecting seven
saffron-robed Masai warriors leaning
on their spears in a clearing
at midnight; a moon-
landing souvenir mug, a slab
of agate on a Chinese chest, my pen-
holder made
from the hide
of a lion.

Chicago, 1969

America developed my commercial streak: I sold
Kool-Aid on our street corner, describing it
to neighbours and passers-by as 'indescribably delicious'.

Whatever happened to the Piles? We all smirked
whenever their name came up. I later
deduced that they were not only nudists, but swingers too.

With Sue and Cindy, and some luminous paint, we transformed
our garden shed into a ghost-house – a dime for kids, adults
a quarter. Its wailing spectres and shivering quicksand

failed to scare their older brother
who was home in Palatine after a weirder
kind of magical mystery tour.

Enter, Fleeing

Undo that step, or at the least
tread softly, for a sleek
and bushy-tailed urban fox
is counting chick-
chick-chick-
chickens in his dreams; when he wakes
he'll yawn
and prowl, while I'll
be staring, shamefaced, down
the grainy, haunted
vistas opened
by insomnia. Sing, birds, I mean all
ye bird-brained in every
furrow that you hop in; warble
tales of the species that will wade
through estuaries, and stalk the plains, or tunnel
beneath them, after mishap
or meteor. Convulsed
and jangling, flooded
with adrenaline, the body empties itself of water
    in order
to skedaddle, to leap
and run ever higher
and faster, only the seconds
pass and each
stretched limb, each trembling joint stays
locked in unremitting combat
with itself. Gulp
or gab, gab, gab, gulp – out
stream the lies, twisting

in the wind, for who
ever felt a single sensation? Is not
everyone at the same moment
conscious that there co-
exist a thousand
others? I flinched when the tongue of the thin
green snake flickered as I slid
through the hedge; American milk
tasted different, while in blurry
black-and-white an eager
villain heaved
his shield at Fluid-Man, who changed, chuckling
aloud, into mist or stream, or slanting
rain. I saw, amazed, a cartoon
needle stitching nametags inscribed
in flaming italics with my own
initials and name
into the waistbands and collars
of unfamiliar clothes; the air
was sucked out
of my lungs, while iridescent specks wriggled
and turned turtle
before my eyes. My brother
was singing of Daniel – he was leaving
tonight on a plane . . . we watched
the red tail lights
at O'Hare, and found that he'd left
behind in our elegantly finned
maroon Chevrolet his equally maroon
school cap, which I
at once hoisted high, and then
with a grimace, and a flourish, put on.

Tribal

Idly scrolling, between
tasks, through some
footie fanatics'
thread, I clicked
on a link, and saw
through a swarm
of settling flies the grubby
and bloodied
profile of Theo Walcott
on an arm thrust
through the window of what
remained of a jeep, and tattooed
beneath him the large-
wheeled cannon that is
our crest.

Viewless Wings

What aileth thee now, that thou art
wholly gone up to the housetops?
　　　　　　　– Isaiah 22 : 1

I (gulp) had
to have a certain operation, and as
I went under, found
myself assailed by a flock
of hostile pigeons, by a whole
parliament of fowls, cooing
hysterically – blackbirds
and ospreys
and screaming gulls. *How daft*
are you! mocked
a jackdaw, jabbing
its beak at my groin. Vile droppings
filled my mouth
and throat, while swallows and wrens
and magpies settled
on my midriff . . . aghast, barely
able to breathe, I stretched
forth a hand and seized
a cormorant's quill
that I plunged
deep into the breast
of a hapless nightingale, all
the while chanting aloud the poor
bird's ode; which, to my surprise, worked. Oh I felt
like Orpheus when their harsh
cawing hushed because my pumping heart
ached – I squawked
and clucked and preened and burst

into song, *tra-la*, at which a malignant
crow keeled over, drowsy,
numb. *Maaaghkk*, screeched a brilliant
green parrot
in my ear, but nothing followed, no
salacious wit. I caught
and caressed a downy gosling – it squirmed
and scratched at first, but soon
enough curled up, a ball
of quivering fluff, and its tiny
heart stopped beating. How
perplexing – for now
I was Orpheus in the underworld, surrounded
by the dead, and my long-sought
Eurydice was a moulting eagle
shrieking at me to turn
around, to let
her be. Twisting,
sliding, I flapped
my leaden wrists and arms and tried
to look ahead, but heard
as my own requiem an owl
hooting mournfully to its mate – *who – who – who –*
killed Cock Robin? . . . he lies
here forlorn, dew
dabbling his breast, down
and out. Let
others mourn and peck, respectfully, at his
remains: we ask – tu-whit
tu-whoo – why
was it his cœur triste *the arrow*
pierced, and why
did he not spy
with his gimlet eye, the impending

peril. Out
of all
he thought might count, this
pinch of dust is about
how much got counted. Therefore
strew larkspur, plant gloomy
sharp-needled evergreens to moan
and sigh when evening's
breezes stir, and ruffle
our feathers as we stretch
our wings and our saucer-
eyes swivel, and these claws
extend, retract, extend and the moon
rises, and we wonder – does he wake
or sleep?

Love Triangle

Here – ahem – is a motif
that has proved
popular in many
diverse cultures
in many eras: think, for instance
of Arthur, Lancelot and Guinevere;
or think
if you dare, of your
own turbid y-y-y-youth.

A Broken Appointment

I opened the envelope: it contained
a ticket in my name from London
St Pancras to Paris Nord, departing at 9.17 on the twelfth
of the twelfth, a Friday; coach 3
seat 27, non-smoking; and another
for returning the following day, at thirteen
minutes past two, in the afternoon – *dans l'après-*
midi; and a postcard of Pierre
Bonnard's *Le Bol de lait*, and there was just
one word on the back – *Come* – followed
by an *x*. Whenever
I pour
a dish of milk, or dwell
on the loop in the C of her
unfamiliar hand, I can't
help thinking – 'Oh
what a poem – what a poem Thomas Hardy
might have written
about this!'

Under the Lime Trees

All that glitters
is not glass, but lots and lots
of it is, mused
the helmeted cyclist . . . O you fast-
spinning tyres, so delicately ridged, so like the scales
of a young crocodile – avoid
whatever sparkles, and that
straggle-haired woman weaving
her way briskly against the traffic, her hands
a jiving blur as she belts
out snatches of *We're just
two little girls from Little Rock . . . the one who broke
my heart . . .*
in Little Rock . . . Are these
I spy the deserving
poor, fully adrift, or breast-fed bohemians (weird
thought of the day!) jostling on a street corner beside
an all but emptied rack
of Boris Bikes? Wolves
living on wind, *sur le Noël, morte
saison . . .*
            we do not feel
the speck of dust that alights
on our shoulder, nor
its fatal cousin, the germ we inhale, unknowing,
and cannot spit out. It slides
through the unmapped city
within. Responsive
cells divide or move, suddenly
restless, alert, driving, dragging

from the abyss an image
of myself cowboy-hatted, aged three, proudly astride
an East African zebra. The spongy marrow
buried in our bones
enriches the blood that unites, as it flows, nerve
and muscle, tissue and tendon, propelling
all smoothly forward like a river swirling
over its unseen bed; while every
active capillary, if challenged, or opposed, or howsoever
aroused, dilates
in bold defiance, in outright
scorn of the cold footsteps creeping like mist . . .
                                        blink,
and click your heels one-two-three, and the yellow
brick road is thigh-
deep in nettles and willowherb. Even
when it's invisible the sun
flings into space its gassy flames, each day
enthrones itself, and we, too, must purge our minds of the inert
and confining, dwell
in thoughts that breathe, and words that burn, or shine
as brightly as a falling
guillotine . . . blink
again and the fantastical
flow of money
and data bursts like a blood vessel, scattering
the crowds gathered beneath the weeping
limes. It happened
I fell in with one kicking wildly
at piles of sticky, heart-shaped leaves – his cheeks were furrowed
with scars, and his left ear seemed torn: 'Follow',
he confided, 'the scent to the vixens' lair . . . take up
your broken bicycle, and with both hands hurl it as far . . .
    as far . . .'

II

Well, we must *be for ourselves in the long run . . .*
— EMILY BRONTË, *Wuthering Heights*

Supply and Demand

'Lord O Lord, not
again,' sighed
the printer who set
Henry David
Thoreau's *Walden*, and kept
running out
of the letter
'I' . . .

Mickey Finn

        . . . I drank
and was surprised
to see what looked like tea leaves
at the bottom
of the cup . . . minutes
later a great warm green wave
or cloud
began advancing towards me. 'Look at the boats
on his shirt,' I felt myself trying
to say, in Spanish, or Arabic, yet knowing
I knew
none of the words . . .

        it was bright
morning, and the train had arrived
and emptied
at Chamartín before I finally
pried open my eyes, and saw
on the carriage floor
nothing but an unfamiliar
pair of trainers: cracked
white leather, with three green stripes. 'Mister –
or rather Herr – Adolf
Dassler made these,' I thought. But which
of the two friendly men with whom
I'd shared the carriage, and some wine,
had been wearing them? I pondered
this awhile, then fell
asleep again . . .

                    and did
Herr Dassler visit, personally, all the cities inscribed
on his trainers? Köln, Dublin, Hamburg, Malmö,
Kopenhagen, Bern, Amsterdam . . . and fit
the trainer to the city? Rom, like these, Wien,
London . . .

                    Señor Dassler, I am dreaming of you
on a bench on a platform in a train station
in Madrid, unable
to wake up, a pair
of your trainers, that weren't mine, but now are,
on my feet . . .

                    I am swimming, Herr
Dassler, in your wake, though I fear
you are dead, a corpse washed clean by the numbing tides
with three slanting stripes emblazoned
on your chest, your passport and your wallet
drifting to the ocean floor . . .

                              I discovered
in a pocket – oh! the kindness
of strangers! – about
forty pesetas; but casting
around for a joke or silver lining, I found
nada – or *niente*, as I put it
to my shoes . . . closing
my eyes, I imagined fingers untying
and easing off my Reeboks, as the train
hurtled through the darkness, the men trying
them on in turn, the ex-owner of these
flexing his toes, padding up and down, nodding
approval. They must have whispered

                         [37]

like parents, as they lifted my shirt and unfastened
my money belt, or perhaps, more like surgeons, they used
scissors, or a knife . . .

                          snicker-snack! I watched
the vorpal blade trace
arabesques across my breastbone, hover, then slide
between two ribs. *Chug-chug*
went the trains. The heat
was building, the potion
at last wearing off. How light
I'd be, I now
began to reason, as quick and canny
as a lizard, a perfectly camouflaged
lizard, who'd shed a skin and acquired a new
way of walking.

Dark Matter

The estuary mud
of the Thames, lit by the wrath of a blood-
red sun, laid bare
the future: in the squelching ooze the river god
sculpted our city
in miniature, moulding the heavy silt
until rooftop and turret and arch lay spread
before us, exact
and glistening; then he swelled
with displeasure, and swept it away
in a swirl
of sediment . . .

*

Dark
matter
that I guessed
was originally jam
came to encrust whatever books he begged,
    or borrowed
or stole. Some
got scribbled in, and some
illuminated: I trace
like a scar the spindly outline of a figure
dwarfed by a collapsing tower
sketched on the title page of *Brideshead
Revisited* . . .

*

                    On loan
to a new media outfit, and holed up
for a week or so in a shivering
hotel in besieged
Aleppo, all communications
down, and the road to Damascus one endless
roadblock, she plunged
both hands into an overflowing
rucksack, rummaged awhile, then hauled
out her, or his, or even my
black-
spined Tacitus . . .

Mayhem

after Tacitus

Gaius Suetonius Paulinus
at that time
controlled Britain. According
to rumour, which loves to pit
one man against another, he had grown deeply envious
of Corbulo, and yearned to equal
his rival's recovery of Armenia
by himself gloriously putting to the sword
some foreign adversary. Therefore, fixing
on the isle of Anglesey, where many refugees
had sought safety, he had constructed an armada
of flat-bottomed boats, and these conveyed
his foot soldiers across the treacherous, shallow
sound. His cavalry had to ford
the cold waters on their mounts, and even,
in the deeper parts, to swim beside their horses.

Along the shore, near
the tideline, men
waited, bristling with weapons, and weaving
between them, women in funereal black
like Furies, hair
hanging down,
brandishing torches. And Druids, everywhere
Druids, shrieking, hands lifted
to the heavens, stunning the invaders with their harrowing
curses . . . dismayed
and paralysed, even the battle-hardened quailed, seemed
almost to offer up their bodies for slaughter; until,

roused by their general, and urging
themselves not to be daunted by a band
of fanatical women, they advanced
and attacked, decimating
all they encountered, slashing and burning, setting
alight the foe with the flames
of their own torches . . . Victory
accomplished, a garrison
was established and the island's
sacred groves razed: for those savages would drown
their altars in human blood, and consult their gods by probing
the entrails of butchered prisoners. It was,
however, while he was busy
accomplishing all this, that Suetonius learned of a sudden
rebellion, of unspeakable
mayhem, of terror engulfing the skeleton
army he'd left to defend
the colony's main province.

Colombo, 1970

Civil war! Peter, urged on, perhaps,
by Simon, broke
a broom on Agnes's head, causing
her blood to flow, and streak
her yellow sari; and yet it was Agnes
who got dismissed: 'She insulted',
my father gruffly explained,
'Peter's mother.'

Simon, Agnes,
Peter – these
were not the names chosen
for Agnes
or Simon
or Peter
at birth.

Stigmata

Oh! Qui veut m'écorcher
– JULES LAFORGUE

Beleaguered fibres, believe me, the oxygen
breathed in
by these lungs is on
its way: the mind, in thrall
to buried rage, will not – will NOT
for once immobilise and stretch
and peg me out as the Lilliputians pegged
out Gulliver; I mean
to ignore this mere
tickle, as of
a stinging nettle, even
as its toxins creep, then surge through my enfeebled
nerves . . . Between
bouts, between
lapses I burn
candles, moxa, incense, hold
postures for minutes
on end; and learn
that the gods of the myoclonic twitch, of the inflamed
larynx, allot
and measure
not only pain, but how it survives
as a tangle
of signs and floating
variables trans-
mitted periodically from cortex
to spine.

After
the jitters, after the pills and insomnia, the weeping
and flipping out, I wandered
around, feeling
flayed. A Daoist
I met in Bremen, fresh
from Eastern travels, explained, and promised
to help me find
my *ziran*, my fluid, untrammelled
inner being. 'Oh Axel,' I countered, 'I'm bones,
jiggling bones in a sack, *y alma*
en boca, and whatever
soul there is, in the mouth.' '*Nein – nein – nein*,'
he replied, 'a river
runs through you: heaven or hell, hide
or seek, hope or despair – Gaia
herself is dying of your binaries. Can you kneel
and beg forgiveness
of bacteria? You fidget, you fail
to answer, *ja*, and I feel
you divide your own heart
into zones – that your past, like a famished
rodent, is beginning to gnaw into ribbons
your future . . .' The cavernous
plaza I fled across
echoed and blended my footsteps with his
parting cries – '*ja* . . . it is *gnawing* . . .
into *ribbons* . . . your *future* . . .'

Hong Kong, 1973

How profusely our parents thanked
the postman who finally delivered, in one
big batch, our carefully scrutinised
weekly letters – letters addressed
not to where they lived, which was 9
Bowen Hill, but to 77 Conway
Court, a wholly fictitious building
we'd invented. O ingenious
postman! – you delved
beneath the words
we wrote, and discovered
what we meant.

Daphne and Apollo

after Ovid

As the chaff in a mown field is suddenly
Ablaze, as flames invade
A parched hedgerow, so the stricken sun-god
Found himself violently on fire
With love for Daphne; his heart,
The marrow deep in his bones, began to ache, then burn.

'Slow down,' he cried out, 'or I will burn
Away! Beloved nymph, I'm no savage wolf suddenly
Bearing down on a lamb, no lion clawing at the heart
Of a deer, no bloodthirsty enemy invading
Its peaceful neighbour. I want only to cherish you, to fire
You with passion fit for the sun-god

Which is who I am: for my father is Jove, god
Of gods, and at my temple in Delphi supplicants burn
Countless offerings, worship ME, master of music, of poetry,
    lord of the fiery
Day-star, dispenser of herbs and potions that effect sudden
Miraculous cures. But you alone can cure the disease invading
Me now, can relieve this terrible pain consuming my heart . . .'

Poor bewildered Daphne fled ever faster, her heart
In her mouth as the infatuated sun-god
Quickened his pace: imagine a hare twisting and turning,
    desperate to evade
A pursuing greyhound – so she feinted between trees,
    his breath burning
Her neck, every second dreading the sudden
Grasp of his hands, the triumph of his pitiless 'fire'.

By the waters of the river Peneus she collapsed, panting:
   'Father, the fire
My beauty has aroused in the heart
Of Apollo is ending my life. End my beauty instead . . .'
   Suddenly
Her limbs were overcome by a strange torpor, and as the eager
   god
Reached for his prey, he felt rings of bark instead of burning
Flesh, found the arms he seized were branches, saw leaves
   invade

Her hair, while her feet lengthened into roots, invading
The soil on which he knelt, weeping. The fire
That had so tortured him altered too, from burning
Desire to gentle affection: caressing the tree's trunk, he yet
   sensed her heart
Retreating from the kisses he showered on her, at which the god
Burst out: 'This sudden

Change as suddenly undoes my longing to invade
With god-like fire your reluctant
Heart. These leaves in my hair are all I need; I burn for you no
   more.'

Bahrain, 1977

On this scorched island in the Gulf, night
after night, I dreamed
of buying, and then mastering
the art of riding
a skateboard; and during
the long
hot afternoons I lay
under a fan and read crumbling
Penguin Classics – *England, My England* –
Lady Chatterley's Lover.

Fide et Literis

Ping! I ponder
another crazed instruction, viz. *climb*
Jacob's Ladder
in the gloaming, and once
aloft, decipher the drift
of the stars
and their freewheeling
constellations – only I can't
bear
to look upwards or back, forwards
or down: moithered
and listless, I need an influx
of what D. H. Lawrence called 'marrow-thought'
to banish the fears
accrued over decades around sacrum
and spine . . . O tell
it not in Gath, but even
while I'm gently pacing
these suburban streets, in sandals
and kaftan, waiting, waiting, watching
for dawn, I'm prone
to the suspicion
that a mad surgeon, needle
and scalpel poised, is on my tail. The cycles
of gibberish swirling
through my mind – *you left*
under a cloud
but I love you! – fade as the heavens
lighten, and a faint
mizzle descends, and fresh

instructions
flood the land.

*

We gazed in wonder
at a bone from the little finger
of Saint Teresa of Ávila: each
and every midnight a seraph
pierced her entrails with a golden spear
at whose tip burned a tiny, wavering flame.

'*Follow me*,' whispered a voice
in the shadows to Saint Jerome, 'for the music
you hear is the music
of the spheres – oh arise, arise
and dance with me, reach forth
and cup my breasts in your hands.'

How those watching in the forum gasped
when the great spiked wheel shivered and groaned
and shattered! – at which, undaunted, firm
in his faith, Maxentius summoned
an executioner, who as firmly
beheaded the wonder-working saint.

Although officially vowed to celibacy, the desert
fathers had desert sons, who in time
acquired their fathers' looks
and habits; their desert mothers instructed
them in Latin, then returned
them to the desert, to the wilderness.

*

The letter killeth, faith survives . . . I dreamt I was walking with Hölderlin down a white, straight road. After several hours of companionable silence I began to question him about the people we had passed on the way, who included my mother and my father, my wife and my daughters. He cocked an eyebrow, and led me to a crag high above the Danube, which he insisted we call by its ancient Greek name of Istros. 'There is a reason', he began, 'that rivers run through dry land. All that is needed is a sign . . .' He harrumphed, and pointed. I stared in the direction of his outstretched index finger, and saw a tower. In the topmost window of the tower was Hölderlin himself, waving.

New York, 1982

A loft on Crosby Street: I thought
to have employed
a bit of Ovid, skilfully
updated, to explain
what happened in it.

Adrift

Colonel Muammar Gaddafi's wife, or rather
widow, recently wrote to me asking for help in transferring
some important financial assets from a secret location: only I,
she insisted, had the expertise to perform this complex operation.

Is there a more ferocious texter than General Pinochet's
daughter? I've no idea how she got my number.
It seems that her fridge-freezer is empty, and her bedroom
bugged; now her toenails need clipping, now she can't find
    her keys.

A minor ex-mistress of Laurent Gbagbo's tweets practically
every day. He, apparently, has become a serious fan
of my poetry. She has a cache of uncut diamonds for sale,
    a terrible
headache most mornings, and a fear of flying in any class
    but first.

I'm just too tired to think of replying to this email
inviting me to go trekking in the Himalayas with a
    distant 'cousin'
of Pervez Musharraf. The gender of this 'cousin' is unclear,
and I fear his – or her – 'invitation' is really a threat.

'You have reached 0207 . . .' my machine was intoning
but I snatched the handset from the cradle; I'd urgent
business with a dude I'd just met – a cool cool
customer called Rafa something something something,
    then definitely

ending in Marcos.

Brighton Rock

I walked beside the seething waves, in shock,
Baffled such chaos had come to *me*;
My heart was in hiding – all I heard was the knock

Of pebble on pebble, the cries of a flock
Of seagulls circling over the sea . . .
I walked beside the seething waves, in shock,

And battered my temples in a fit of mock
Self-punishment, wanting others to see
That my heart, in hiding, heard only the knock

Of pain, thought of time as a clock
Ripped apart, yet ticking remorselessly,
As I walked beside the seething waves, in shock,

And watched a crab crawl over a rock
Waving its pincers merrily –
But my heart, in hiding, heard only the knock

Of anger, saw the future as a door whose lock
An axe or machete must open, there being no key.
Yes, my heart was in hiding, until I heard its *knock-
    knock-knock*
As I walked beside the seething waves, in shock.

Oxford, 1985

Oh to recapture the golden summer
I met Allen Ginsberg! That tireless man! – he had
within minutes produced
a whole box of photographs of himself, all shaggy
and naked, in bed
with a blond admirer. Had
he taken these pictures himself? I enquired, marvelling
at their composition . . . he had!

Trial and Error

I am not all Heere
– JOHN DONNE

Tired of the eighties, and the on-
going crisis in masculinity – the compliment
each generation pays itself – he stared
a hole in his macchiato,
fished with his spoon
beneath the froth. The hiss
and gurgle of steam heating milk, the grinding
of beans he heard as souls
departing; his own
strained for glimpses of moon-
faced babies, pink-jowled noble savages without
– ha-ha – even
a shoe size, unable to feed
or to clean themselves, to interrupt
their gulping and wailing. 'I find
your beauty unsettling . . .' – had
he *really* said that to the girl carrying
a purple yoga mat? Why
is it the healthy in body and mind
discover each other? – likewise
the maimed? More
or less at random, dollops
of unfairness are gathered, braided and put
to use, until a dooms-
day scenario emerges, and the lungs
heave like broken bellows, erratic, desperate,
constrained . . .

*

Dear Agony
    Aunt, I am wading
        through bodies, searching
            for mine, convinced
                it must
                    be here, surrounded
                        by flowers, not a hair
                            out of place.

Dear Agony
    Aunt, the righteous
        and the self-righteous
            are swarming
                through my brain and I can't
                    tell them apart
                        I can't tell
                            them apart.

Dear Agony
    Aunt, there are three
        hundred million guns
            in America, so isn't
                it important that we wear
                    industry-approved
                        and securely fitted
                            body armour at all times?

Dear Agony
   Aunt, when the agony
      abates, how should I
         spend my time now
            that I no longer
               fish, and, in your
                  opinion, when do you think
                     it will start again?

Dear Agony
   Aunt, we keep finding
      'Dear Agony
         Aunt' notes all
            over the house,
               in our closets and laundry, beneath
               our pillows, in bright
                  lipstick on mirrors.

Dear Agony
   Aunt, please excuse
      my engrossing so much
         of your attention – although since
            you barely ever reply why
               on earth should I worry? – but I
               have a problem
                  that won't go away.

*

In dreamy Pensão
Liberdade your eczema
and night terrors subsided, but in dingy
Pensão Castelo they flared
up again. How aware, I wondered
aloud, of each other are the catastrophes
waiting so impatiently
to engulf us? There is, with a flick
of bangles and ponytail
you replied, a corner of hell where the flippant
writhe and attack themselves, consumed by wolf-
fanged remorse; we both
know that ignorance
can be no
less structured than knowledge. I may
be guessing here, but was it
my sewing scissors or the gadget for peeling
potatoes that you used
to trim your thinning hair? Heart, take
five – my chakras
are fizzing, each
one warning of your fearful eagerness to strip
away the essential
me; how do you, we keep
puzzling, how *can*
you carry on through it all, like a water- or a waste-
pipe-fall?

*

Alone, unobserved,
    the octopus broods
        within its brown
           wicker pot.

Thwack! – a cross-legged monk
    welcomes the fall
        of bamboo
           on bare shoulders.

The din of crickets; I bought
    leeks, dried
        salmon, wandered
           through withered fields.

Notes

'Aloft' makes use of the prose poem 'Le Port' by Charles Baudelaire.

'Tribal': Theo Walcott played for Arsenal from 2006 to 2018.

'Mickey Finn': the German sports company Adidas was founded by Adolf Dassler. In the late 1970s and early 1980s Adidas released a range of trainers named after European cities.

'Mayhem' is adapted from a passage in book 14 of *Annales* by Tacitus.

'Hong Kong, 1973': 'carefully scrutinised'. It was often a rule in British boarding schools of the 1970s that all letters had to be read through by a member of staff before being posted.

'Daphne and Apollo' derives from Ovid's *Metamorphoses*, book 1, lines 492–565.